MW00715348

Judy & Henry,

Thankes Thanks, Thanks
for leading the way
in one exception to
remake Kevin |K|
Guest |G|
House |H|
Peace / Love,
Tom Garvey

KEVIN
GUEST HOUSE
GERALD L. HALLIGAN
FOREWORD BY DENIS GARVEY

Thank you for your support
of Kevin Guest House.
Gerald L. Halligan
8/25/16

ARCADIA
PUBLISHING

Published by Arcadia Publishing
Charleston, South Carolina

Printed in the United States of America

Library of Congress Control Number: 2015959878

For all general information, please contact Arcadia Publishing:
Telephone 843-853-2070
Fax 843-853-0044
E-mail sales@arcadiapublishing.com
For customer service and orders:
Toll-Free 1-888-313-2665

Visit us on the Internet at www.arcadiapublishing.com

*To the perpetual spirit of Cyril and Claudia Garvey, which
lives on through services provided by Kevin Guest House.*

Images of Modern America

KEVIN
GUEST HOUSE

CONTENTS

FOREWORD

A family home is a very special place. It is built to provide shelter but serves a much greater purpose.

The home is where a family grows close through shared experiences of love and joy and heartache. It's where children learn real-life lessons from parents not just by what they say but by what they do.

My father, Cyril Garvey, once said, "If you are lucky enough to have just one good idea and work really hard on it, it makes life all worthwhile." The house at 782 Ellicott Street Buffalo, New York, was just such an idea.

Built by the Fisher family in the late 1800s, it was then purchased by Theophilus and Ernestine Speyser in 1904. The Speyser family and, later, their in-laws of the Louis Beer family lived in the house until 1970.

Cyril and Claudia Garvey lost their 13-year-old son, my brother Kevin to leukemia in January 1972. Our home was in Pennsylvania, but Kevin's treatment was at Roswell Park Memorial Hospital. During their many stays in Buffalo, my mother and father recognized the financial burden of affordable shelter other parents were experiencing while caring for their loved ones also being treated at Roswell. They purchased the house at 782 Ellicott Street and, in July 1972, opened its doors as a home away from home for families in need.

Imbued with the spirits of all of its past family's sorrows and joys, this home now called Kevin Guest House has become a beacon of hope providing shelter, comfort, and understanding to those in times of incredible need.

—Denis Garvey

ACKNOWLEDGMENTS

From the beginning of this project, some individuals have asked why I decided to write about the founding of Kevin Guest House. The simple explanation is my former editor at Arcadia Publishing had a conversation with Suzy Garvey in 2013, and he asked me to go to learn about the facility. From that first visit, the compulsion to write about Kevin Guest House seemed to be inevitable.

Grateful thanks goes to the Garvey family, notably Tom Garvey, who listened to my proposal for the book and provided invaluable suggestions for its early development. In later research, Denis and Suzy Garvey provided critical insight that could not be gleaned from the local sources. This included significant family documentation and facts related to the establishment of Kevin Guest House.

The author is grateful for support from past and present staff. Grateful thanks go to former executive directors Jen Ann Berger and Wayne Zimmerman; current executive director Lynsey Zimdahl Weaver has been actively involved in discussions on the book's contents, setting up appointments, reaching out to past associates, and reviewing the final layouts for the book. Additional thanks go to her staff members Courtney Jensen, Pam Chrzanowski, Kate Heidinger, and Jeff Davis for their assistance.

Many thanks are extended to current board president Kevin Durawa and previous board members and staff members Dean Drew, Neil Farmelo, Karen Synor, Aimee Gomlak, Barbara Fraser, Fred Vosburgh, Darlene Spychala, Amy Vigneron, Andrew Banchich, and many others.

Thanks go to the administration and staff of Roswell Park Cancer Institute for information and photographs—especially to Dr. Edwin A. Mirand, who provided details on the history of the institute.

The author extends long-distance thanks to Karylinn Echols of the Healthcare Hospitality Network for historical archive material. Also, thanks go to contributing Hospitality House administrators and staff from around the nation; these people include Lauren Zamora, Ronald McDonald House, Philadelphia, Pennsylvania; Mona Johnson-Gibson and Vicky Seksinsky of Ronald McDonald House of Charlotte, North Carolina; Carrie Howell, Hospitality House of Charlotte, North Carolina; and Ann Raderman of Hope Lodge, Buffalo, New York.

Special thanks are extended to the Speyser-Beer family for granting permission to include the early history of the original owners of the property: Claudia Beer Rodgers, Vanessa Beer Korn, Barbara Beer Rendall, and Richard Beer.

Among the volunteers, guests and supporters of Kevin Guest House who granted interviews, images, and reviewed historical facts are Roz Annunizato, Lucy McCabe, and Renee Lorek.

Thanks go to Jennifer Lynne Smith for technical and photographic assistance and Monica Bruce to photographic contributions. Thanks also go to Kathleen M. Halligan for patience and support throughout this project.

Unless otherwise noted, all images appear courtesy of Kevin Guest House Archives. Please note that Roswell Park Memorial Hospital became Roswell Park Cancer Institute in 1992 and Buffalo General Hospital became Buffalo General Medical Center in 2012.

INTRODUCTION

The beliefs and optimism of a young doctor forged in 1897 merged with the beliefs of a family from Pennsylvania during July 1970 in Buffalo, New York.

Cyril and Claudia Garvey of Sharon, Pennsylvania brought their son Kevin to the Memorial Hospital in Buffalo, which was named after its founder, Dr. Roswell Park. Their deep love for the child along with unwavering faith carried them through and beyond the medical interventions during an 18-month period in the early 1970s. This would include a trip to the Sanctuary of Our Lady of Lourdes in France, seeking a miraculous cure for Kevin's illness.

The chronicle of the Garvey family's struggle is imbedded in a transition period for the hospital and the city of Buffalo during the turbulent 1960s. Although the Garveys had financial means, it was clear that many other parents seeking treatment for their children were not as fortunate. Compelled by this troubling fact, they sought to create an option for others, even though Kevin's treatment was their primary concern when traveling to Buffalo, New York.

Although the Garveys were resourceful individuals of strong character, help was needed to create a solution, which was desperately needed, for they observed that families whose children had life-threatening diseases would need long-term lodging, emotional support, and financial relief. Fortunately, they were able to attract like-minded advocates to address these problems, common to many coming Roswell Park Cancer Institute and other hospitals.

The Garveys' concern for others during their own time of suffering is a model of active compassion. One former board member commented, "The death of a child, a horrible tragedy, became a wellspring of their inspiration." Thus, the result of their collective influence, Kevin Guest House, opened in July 1972 and has remained in service for over 40 years. Just how that was accomplished, despite very difficult financial constraints, has been a major factor throughout the research interviews conducted for this book.

The opening chapter explores the original owners of the property and the features of houses within the Fruit Belt of Buffalo. Chapter 2 follows with a brief pictorial profile of the child, Kevin, whom most supporters of the house have only seen in his iconic painting.

Chapters 3 through 8 provide highlights of the circumstances about the founding of the Kevin Guest House, its physical transformation, and its impact on other individuals and communities throughout the United States.

With the need for Hospital Hospitality Houses continuing to grow across the country, Kevin Guest House will steadfastly remain a special place within the Buffalo Niagara Medical Campus. This book is intended to raise awareness and support this local institution and its noble mission.

One

THE ORIGINAL OWNERS
OF THE PROPERTY

Seen here is formal portrait of the Speyser family, who owned the property at 782 Ellicott Street, Buffalo, New York, from 1904 to 1971. From left to right are Clara Speyser, eldest daughter (1881–1958); Ernestine Speyser, mother (1857–1936); Louis T. Speyser, son (1873–1956); Mathilda Speyser, daughter (1885–1969), and Theophil Speyser, father (1845–1913). (Courtesy of the Speyser-Beer family.)

Theophil and Ernestine Speyser are shown here by the flower bed in front of their home at 782 Ellicott Street, Buffalo, New York, in early 1900s. Theophil was born on October 1, 1845, in Reichenweir (now Riquewihr), Upper Alsatia, France, and emigrated to the United States, settling in Buffalo in 1870. His wife, Ernestine Lacroix, was from Friedrichsthal, Baden, Germany. (Courtesy of the Speyser-Beer family.)

Theophil Speyser gained prominence among German manufacturers in Buffalo. He had applied his cabinetmaking skills in several local communities before returning to the city of Buffalo around 1879. After opening his own coffin and furniture-making company, and purchasing an established coffin factory, Speyser incorporated Buffalo Trunk Manufacturing in 1906. Today, the factory building at 127–130 Cherry Street is listed in National Register of Historic Places (Courtesy of the Speyser-Beer family.)

This is the Victorian-style house at 782 Ellicott Street, Buffalo, New York, in 1906, that became Kevin Guest House. Several prominent citizens going back to the early 1800s owned the property. In 1865, the land was deeded to Jacob P. Fisher, who was in the brewing business. The house was constructed around 1869. The Speyser family purchased the house in 1904. (Courtesy of the Speyser-Beer family.)

This is a close-up view of the porch of the Speysers home in 1907. The German families of this area enhanced their properties with plants and fruit trees. This area became known as the Fruit Belt. Notice the wire trellises attached to the railings on the porch. Standing are, from left to right, Theophilus, Louis (son), Clara (daughter), and Ernestine Speyser. (Courtesy of the Speyser-Beer family.)

This photograph was taken in the backyard of 782 Ellicott Street in May 1907. The view is of the left corner facing Ellicott Street. The open area near the stairway was later enclosed. The two people seen here are unidentified. (Courtesy of the Speyser-Beer family.)

This second photograph of the rear of 782 Ellicott Street details the right corner of the house facing Ellicott Street. In later years, extensive interior remodeling would alter this stairway. The identity of the two individuals could not be confirmed, but family members believe they are the Speyser children. (Courtesy of the Speyser-Beer family.)

In this image is a beautiful winter scene of the front of the Speyser home captured on February 2, 1908. This view gives one a sense of the neighborhood in that time. The front door of the house held two stained-glass windows by prominent artists of the late 1800s. The people fashionably attired for the Buffalo cold are believed to be Ernestine Speyser and her grown children. (Courtesy of the Speyser-Beer family.)

This complementary view from the front yard was taken over the fence and looks toward houses across Ellicott Street from the Speyer home at 782 Ellicott Street on February 2, 1908. Over the ensuing decades, this neighborhood would be transformed by the expansion of both Buffalo General Hospital and Roswell Park Memorial Institute campuses. (Courtesy of the Speyser-Beer family.)

These are the two stained-glass windows that were originally in the front door of 782 Ellicott Street in Buffalo, New York. Between the death of Mathilda Speyser-Beer in 1969 and the sale of the house to Cyril Garvey in 1971, the windows were taken to a Beer family residence in Michigan. Members of the Beer family recall that the windows were in the door when Theophil and Ernestine Speyser purchased the house in 1904. The windows were a source of curiosity and wonder for the Beer grandchildren. The individuals depicted in the stained-glass windows may be the composer Beethoven and the poet William Cullen Bryant. Professional documentation of the glass artist(s) or manufacturer has not been confirmed. (Photographs by the author, courtesy of the Speyser-Beer family.)

Mathilda Speyser accepted a proposal of marriage from Louis H. Beer (1885–1979) in 1914. With the recent death of her husband, Theophil, mother Ernestine asked Mathilda and her fiancé to consider living in the family home following their marriage. This was agreed upon, and Ernestine ordered extensive remodeling of the structure, including installation of a wall to divide the house. Mathilda was married in 1915 and moved into one side of the house. This photograph shows Mathilda with son Robert in 1916. (Courtesy of the Speyser-Beer family.)

Louis H. Beer established a business called Buffalo Leather Goods, which complemented his father-in-law's own company, Buffalo Trunk. It was located at 364 Main Street in downtown Buffalo. This photograph was taken on September 22, 1917. The child in the truck is a one-year-old cousin from California, Charles Beer. The man standing to the left is unidentified. (Courtesy of the Speyser-Beer family.)

In 1959, members of the Speyser-Beer family gather at 782 Ellicott Street in Buffalo. Pictured are, from left to right, (first row) Mabel Stuckie (aunt), Florence Beer; Barbara, Claudia, and Richard Beer (children of Robert and Florence); (second row) Robert Beer, Ella Hoffman (friend), Clara Speyser, Mathilda Speyser-Beer, and Rena Beer (Edward's wife). (Courtesy of the Speyser-Beer family.)

Although unknown to the respective families, within this time period of 1958–1959, a child was born in Sharon, Pennsylvania, who would merge their lives. Kevin Garvey, the seventh child of Cyril and Claudia Garvey, was born in June 1958. He is shown here at one month old with his grandmother Catherine Evans.

Two

A Child from Pennsylvania

Kevin Joseph Garvey was born June 5, 1958, to Cyril T. and Claudia Garvey (née Evans) of Sharon, Pennsylvania. The boy was the seventh of eight children.

This photograph was taken during Kevin Garvey's first Christmas, at home in Sharon, Pennsylvania, in December 1958. Claudia, his mother, is seated in front of the high chair while Cyril, his father, stands alongside.

This photograph was taken in May 1960. Kevin stands among his brothers, sisters, and the family dog, Lucy. Pictured are, from left to right, Tom, Hugh, Mary, Denis, John, and Annette. It is fitting that Denis has his hands placed on Kevin's shoulders, for as he succumbed to his illness, Kevin died in Denis's arms. (Courtesy of the Garvey family.)

Several years later, sister Margaret Garvey would be born and complete Cyril and Claudia's family. From left to right are (first row, seated) Seated, a smiling Kevin, Cyril Garvey, Claudia Garvey (holding Margaret), and Hugh; (second row) Annette, John, Mary, Denis, and Tom.

Kevin is in his mother's arms while she kneels next to Great Aunt May. The album caption from which this photograph was taken notes that she was Kevin's great-grandmother's sister and the last of her family lineage when the photograph was taken.

A smiling Kevin at three years old visits the family's lake house at Pymatuning Lake in Pennsylvania. Cyril Garvey purchased the property in 1960. Over the years, it has become a place of special significance for the Garvey families and their friends.

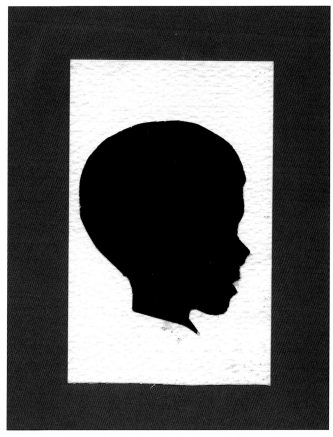

This silhouette of Kevin, along with this crayon drawing by him, were stapled together and attached to a page in a special album put together by his mother. The drawing was the cover decoration for a program sheet for a class performance by Mrs. Frazier's Kindergarten class at S.H. Hadley School in Sharon, Pennsylvania. The play was entitled *A Visit to Mother Goose Land*. There was a morning and an afternoon presentation. Kevin was cast as Peter Peter, as in the nursery rhyme, in the afternoon performance.

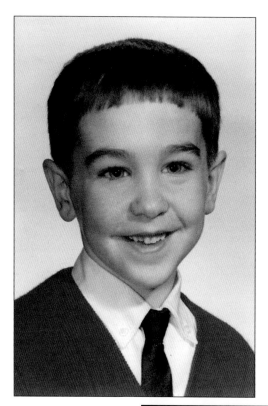

This school portrait of Kevin was taken during first grade at St. Joseph School in Sharon, Pennsylvania, for the 1964–1965 school year. It was his family who gave him his nickname "Heart" during a trip to Niagara Falls in 1966. The doctors, nurses, and staff that cared for Kevin during his medical treatments at Roswell used this nickname.

Kevin enjoyed the holiday costumes that were made for all the children by Claudia Garvey. The caption that accompanies this photograph in his special album states, "If I hadn't smiled, no one would have known me!"

Little Kevin is seen here with his pal Margaret. Kevin's father wrote eloquently about his son in later years: "A most simple child, the most straightforward, and willing to trust in God's providence." A testimonial to that effect is the dedication of a book published in 1972 by Dom Hubert Van Zeller shortly after Kevin had died. The book is titled *Leave Your Life Alone*, and the dedication reads, "For Claudia and Cy in memory of Kevin." (Courtesy of the Garvey family.)

Kevin and Margaret are pictured at Christmas in 1967. An anecdote about Kevin, as told by his father, involves the only transgression by the young boy that he could ever recall. Cyril and Kevin were playing a game of pool when Kevin deliberately scratched. It appeared that Kevin might beat his father, so he pretended he had not meant to do it. Such was his nature; he could not bear to see his father beaten in anything, even if it meant losing himself. (Courtesy of the Garvey family.)

Kevin, with suitcase in hand, prepares to leave for a summer camp at Camp Notre Dame in Fairview, Pennsylvania, in July 1967. Kevin's own written words express his experience very well; most notable is his concern for the construction of the porch at the family's lake house.

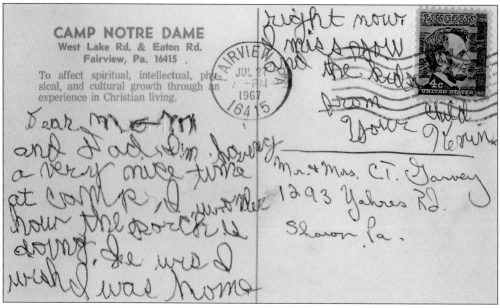

This is a photograph of the entire Garvey family leaving on a trip to Europe in 1966. Kevin is on the right, wearing a plaid jacket and waving in front of his father. Later, in 1971, Cyril, Claudia, and Kevin returned to Europe to visit the shrine at Lourdes, France, for a second time. His father later wrote, "Never to have known such faith and such trust in a child, or for that matter, in an adult." (Courtesy of the Garvey family.)

During sixth grade (1969–1970), Kevin took musical instrument instruction. On July 28, 1970, Kevin and his parents arrived at Roswell Park Memorial Institute in Buffalo to begin his treatments for leukemia. One of the physicians at Roswell who had cared for Kevin later wrote, "Although he [Kevin] had at times difficult periods, he never changed in his relationship to me or his other friends at Roswell. It was as though he was always the master of himself." (Courtesy of the Garvey family.)

25

Seen here is a favorite image of Kevin Joseph Garvey in his baseball uniform. His parents' sentiments for their beloved son are expressed simply: "In the eighteen months that Kevin lived with the illness, that finally conquered even his stout heart, he served constantly as a model and an example for all of us." Kevin passed on to his final reward on January 14, 1972. (Courtesy of the Garvey family.)

Three

THE FIRST HOSPITAL HOSPITALITY HOUSE

The Garveys' arrival at the cancer treatment center at Roswell Park Memorial Institute was in July 1970. In a public presentation by the Garveys in February 1978, they recalled the hospital as being in an old section of Buffalo that was in the early stages of redevelopment. The neighborhood surrounding the hospital consisted of a number of homes in poor repair, with many marked for demolition. (Courtesy of Buffalo State College Archives and Special Collections.)

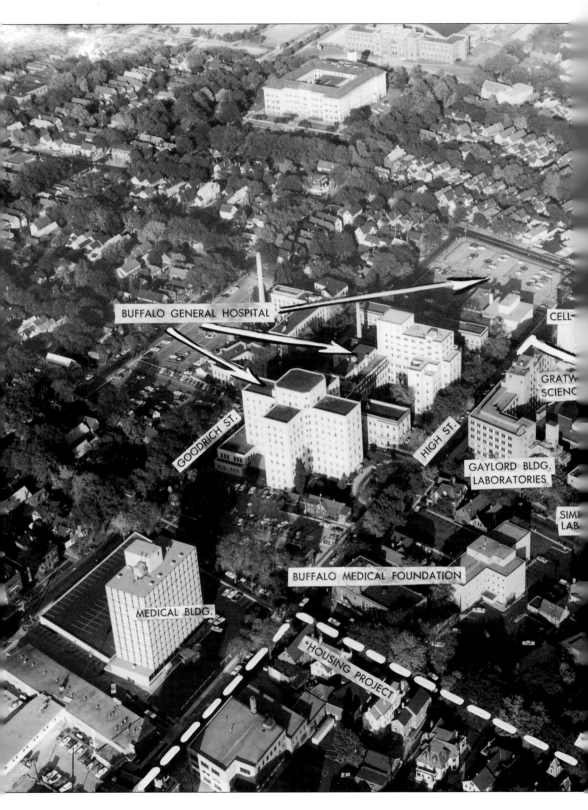

BUFFALO GENERAL HOSPITAL

CELL-

GRATW
SCIENC

GOODRICH ST.

HIGH ST.

GAYLORD BLDG.
LABORATORIES

SIMI
LAB

BUFFALO MEDICAL FOUNDATION

MEDICAL BLDG.

*HOUSING PROJECT

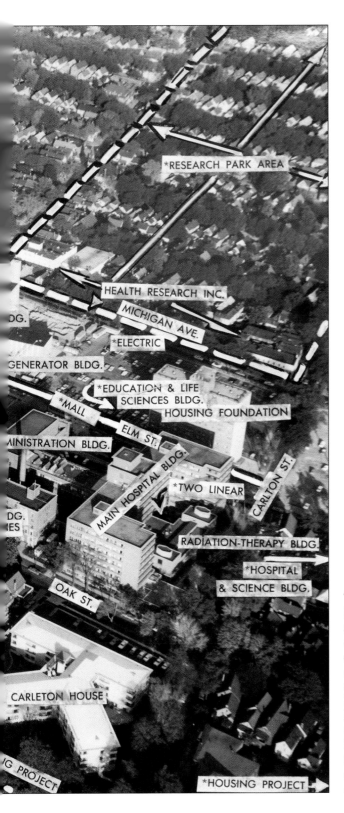

*RESEARCH PARK AREA

HEALTH RESEARCH INC.

MICHIGAN AVE.

*ELECTRIC

DG.

GENERATOR BLDG.

*EDUCATION & LIFE
SCIENCES BLDG.

HOUSING FOUNDATION

*MALL

ELM ST.

INISTRATION BLDG.

MAIN HOSPITAL BLDG.

*TWO LINEAR

CARLTON ST.

DG.
IES

RADIATION-THERAPY BLDG.

*HOSPITAL
& SCIENCE BLDG.

OAK ST.

CARLETON HOUSE

IG PROJECT

*HOUSING PROJECT

This photograph shows the Roswell Park Memorial Institute and surrounding medical-residential complex in December 1984. It details a proposed plan for massive expansion, which includes a controversial expressway. The dotted lines encompass the project areas. Kevin Guest House is between the two "Housing Project" labels at the bottom, center of the photograph. (Photograph by Hoffman Air Photo, courtesy of Buffalo State College Archives and Special Collections.)

29

This is the Cell and Virus Building at the Roswell Institute, completed in 1965. With Roswell being among the top research facilities in the United States at the time, Kevin was able to receive a new experimental drug during his first hospitalization in 1970. Although the initial results were startling, Kevin experienced frequent swings in remissions to relapses. Over time, it became more difficult to provide even a partial remission. (Courtesy of Buffalo State College Archives and Special Collections.)

One of the massive 45,000-gallon oil tanks being installed at Roswell Park Memorial Institute is pictured in June 1965. Along with the Roswell Institute's reputation for innovation in medical advances, it was known for its architects and engineers who undertook one of the largest fuel tank installations ever done in Western New York. (Courtesy of Buffalo State College Archives and Special Collections.)

This is one of the neighborhood blocks near Carlton and Michigan Streets in Buffalo, New York, near Roswell Hospital. This photograph was taken in August 1964 to accompany a newspaper article about the hardships facing residents who were swiftly being displaced. It might well be described as a miracle that the structures, which evolved into the Kevin Guest House campus, were secured by the cooperative efforts of the Garveys and the administration of Roswell at that time. (Courtesy of Buffalo State College Archives and Special Collections.)

This photograph shows Dr. Hollis S. Ingraham (left), New York State health commissioner, and Dr. Gerald P. Murphy at the twin-cornerstone laying ceremony for the buildings of the Comprehensive Drug Center on September 24, 1971. Dr. Murphy, director of the institute—along with Virginia Brady, director of social services, and the Reverend Edward J. Ulaseski, of St. Jude's Center—led a support committee to help the Garveys accomplish their vision of a Hospital Hospitality House. (Photograph by Fred J. Schifferle, courtesy of Buffalo State College Archives and Special Collections.)

The house at 782 Ellicott Street is pictured as Cyril Garvey and Virginia Brady, his advocate from Roswell, would have seen it in December 1971. Negotiations with the Beer family for its sale had begun in March 1971, while an agreement was reached in May 1971. Legal renegotiation with Buffalo Urban Renewal Agency and the City of Buffalo delayed the final approvals until November 1971. The closing was completed on January 5, 1972. Kevin died nine days later. (Courtesy of Buffalo State College Archives and Special Collections.)

The Cummings house, located at 774 Ellicott Street, was photographed by Cyril Garvey between 1971 and 1972. This house sat on the parcel immediately to the left of 782 Ellicott Street. As the circumstances developed, the house was not purchased until 1976. Unfortunately, needed renovations proved to be costly and problematic, so the house was razed. A parking lot currently occupies the property.

This is the second of three color photographs taken by Cyril Garvey of the three buildings adjacent to 782 Ellicott Street. This is at 788 Ellicott Street and was nicknamed "the Little Red School House" due its redbrick exterior at the time. The house was once owned by the Spoth family. They built the carriage apartments over the original garage that is deep in the rear of the property.

This photograph of 788 Ellicott Street was taken in April 1974 as part of series to be used with a newspaper article about Kevin Guest House. The board of directors used this building for different purposes during this time. It was renovated in early 1990s. This led to an innovative and collaborative use of the building implemented by the Roswell Institute and Kevin Guest House: the bone marrow transplant apartments. (Courtesy of Buffalo State College Archives and Special Collections.)

This view of the carriage apartments garage building was taken from the driveway by Cyril Garvey. This structure and its house at 788 Ellicott Street as well as 744 Ellicott Street were purchased together through the auspices of the Buffalo Urban Renewal Agency and the City of Buffalo. This legal process continued well into 1977.

Guests of Kevin Guest House enjoy the accommodations in April 1974. The house was approaching its second anniversary and would celebrate its first formal social event, the Kevin Ball, later that year. Exterior repairs along with interior furnishings were obtained through the generosity of local donors and the fundraising efforts of the Pink Ladies volunteer organization affiliated with Roswell Park Memorial Institute. (Courtesy of Buffalo State College Archives and Special Collections.)

Four

THE CAMPUS

This aerial captures the three principle buildings of the Kevin Guest House campus in winter 2004. In this view looking westward toward the Niagara River, one can appreciate the variety of vintage and modern architecture found in Buffalo, New York.

The history of Kevin Guest House must include the advantage of its proximity to two major hospitals in Buffalo, New York: the Buffalo General Hospital, founded in 1858, and the Roswell Park Cancer Institute, founded in 1897. In a letter to the Garvey family, Dr. Lucius Sinks of Roswell's pediatrics department credits Kevin Guest House's location by Roswell Institute with helping change the medical protocols for cancer patients in the 1970s. He explained that patients who otherwise would have to be admitted to the hospital could receive treatment as outpatients. (Photographs by J.L. Smith, author's collection.)

This detailed photograph of the main building of the Kevin Guest House campus was taken in 2015. Although it features the Victorian style of architecture, extensive interior and exterior modifications have been made during different phases of its occupancy.

Kevin Guest House

Est. 1972

Our Nation's First Hospital Hospitality House
782 Ellicott Street Buffalo, New York
Founded by Attorney Cyril T. and Claudia E. Garvey of Sharon, Pennsylvania

Our Mission is to provide dignity and shelter to families and patients traveling great distances for medical care and treatment in Buffalo, New York.

Mr. & Mrs. Garvey founded the home as a memorial to their 13 year old son Kevin Joseph Garvey, whose nickname was "Heart." He died of leukemia January 14, 1972. Kevin Guest House (KGH) is located in the "heart" of the Buffalo Niagara Medical Campus, one of the premier medical and research centers in the country, where Kevin received treatment at Roswell Park Cancer Institute for 18 months. KGH serves over 1,000 guests annually and is proud to have provided hospitality to guests from 49 of our great United States and many foreign countries from Canada to China.

Many 19th century residences were demolished in the 1970's and 1980's to make way for the expansion of the Buffalo Niagara Medical Campus, which sits on the edge of Buffalo's downtown core. The KGH main house remains one of the last examples of post-Civil War homes on the western edge of Buffalo's historic and oldest residential neighborhood. It was known as the Fruit Belt for it's abundance of orchards left by the area's first settlers.

The house was built in 1885 by Jacob P. Fisher, owner of one of Buffalo's most popular malt houses. In 1904 the Speyser family purchased and lived at 782 Ellicott Street along with their three children. The Speyser family continued ownership until the sale in 1972 to Cyril and Claudia Garvey, when it became the nation's first hospital hospitality house.

788 Ellicott Street, to the north of the Main House, was built around 1868 in the Italianate style; set on a deep lot capable of supporting a garden or a cow. Recognized as workers' housing, the form of this building is historically associated with Buffalo's large working-class immigrant communities, mostly German, Polish, and Irish families. Today this building is used to provide lodging for bone marrow transplant patients and large groups of extended families. Kevin Guest House is a home away from home and welcomes all guests in their time of need.

This historical marker is found in front of Kevin Guest House at 782 Ellicott Street in Buffalo, New York. It was commissioned by the Garvey family. Denis, Tom, and Hugh Garvey were present at the dedication ceremony in July 2014. (Photograph by J.L. Smith, author's collection.)

This view of the north side of the main house of 782 Ellicott Street faces the bone marrow transplant building, located at 788 Ellicott Street.

The front porch of Kevin Guest House is seen here on a sunny morning in August 2015. The beautiful chairs and matching bench with the heart motif are truly enjoyed by the guests. These are enhanced by plants that are maintained by a dedicated group of volunteers. (Photographs by J.L. Smith, author's collection.)

The front room in Kevin Guest House, in which visitors are greeted and guests gather to relax following visitations to the nearby hospitals, is seen here. Furnishings and decor have been carefully selected for the comforts of the guests by staff and donors.

This view looks through the doorway between the front room and the dining room. The staff and volunteers strive on a daily basis to maintain a homelike atmosphere with the entire house. The guests often express how important this is to maintaining their composure under the difficult circumstances that they are facing.

Coming up the stairs from the office side of the main house, guests can rest in bedroom no. 12. From here, one can proceed down the hall toward the front of the house facing Ellicott Street. This room was lovingly renovated through a donation from the Eastman Foundation on July 26, 2012. Also, a small plaque (on the door) features a dedication to the memory of Judith Hughes Babcock.

This is bedroom no. 9. Each room has its own design. Some endowments are given by local organizations while others are chosen by private families to remember their loved ones. This room honors the memory of Henry and Marie Gorino, beloved parents and grandparents of Henry and Christian Gorino. (Photograph by J.L. Smith, author's collection.)

Room no. 7 is referred to as the "Dream Room" by staff and guests. The room was updated through a fundraising event in February 2006, "Ladies Night Out," organized by Katy and Joseph Curotolo and Kelly and Jamie Rehak. Posted on the door is a small donation plague remembering George F. Lamm of American Legion Post No. 622 Auxiliary in 1998. (Photograph by J.L. Smith, author's collection.)

The small plaque on the wall in the "Dream Room" (no. 7) remembers Nina Renay Jones of Pennsylvania, who died at Kevin Guest House on August 16, 2011. Nina was the honored recipient of the Heart of Courage Award in 2006. The room continues to create special significance for many who stay there. This was Nina's favorite room. (Photograph by J.L. Smith, author's collection.)

The kitchen area was renovated in 2009. The staff strives to maintain a clean, well-stocked pantry so that guests can prepare meals for themselves. Sharing one's story in a comfortable place with someone willing to listen can make a big difference for a person trying to cope with a long-term hospitalization. One guest shared that her child's second hospitalization required a stay at Kevin Guest House for 11 months.

Taking the rear stairs near the garage next to the main house, the guests walk out in to the Healing Garden created in 2005 behind the house. Volunteers have helped enhance and maintain this beautiful space over the last 10 years.

Former executive director Wayne Zimmerman was interested in having a garden for the guests to find solace during their stays. Volunteers David (or "Dave") and Katherine Carlson, assisted by Timothy (or "Tim") and Matt Nolan, took on the project. Matt's involvement helped fulfill the requirements in attaining the rank of Eagle Scout. (Photograph by Madison Rose Stranahan, courtesy of David Carlson.)

Garry Valentine, a friend of the Carlsons, designed the location of the beds and the plantings to be used. Dave, Tim, and Matt stripped the area where the beds were to be placed and moved over 17 cubic yards of topsoil into place. (Photograph by J.L. Smith, courtesy of David Carlson.)

The "Heart Houses" on poles were designed by Carrie Nolan Sarafin and built by Justin Takas. The poles were installed after the low-voltage lighting. Carrie also designed the heart images found in the pathway leading to the gazebo. (Photograph by J.L. Smith, courtesy of David Carlson.)

The shrubs, trees, and flowers called for in the plan were installed in the beds. Dave, Tim, and Matt leveled, top-dressed, and seeded the entire grass area and installed the walkway to the Gazebo. Thus, angels can take many different forms to help the guests at Kevin Guest House. (Photograph by J.L. Smith, courtesy of David Carlson.)

While returning to their rooms, the guests are able to view three of the principal buildings on the Kevin Guest House campus with the majesty of the Buffalo General Hospital in the distance. This view from the rear garden is certainly very different than the photograph taken in 1907 shown in chapter 1. (Photograph by J.L. Smith, author's collection.)

Leaving the main house at Kevin Guest House back in the early 1990s, a guest would have seen the side of the Little Red School House building, next door at 788 Ellicott Street. The Buffalo General Hospital, a short distance away on High Street, has had several structural changes to its facade throughout the last 40 years.

This is the view walking to the front of 788 Ellicott Street back in the 1990s. The house did have some basic repairs and maintenance after it was first purchased by the Kevin Guest House organization. However, it was not until this time that major upgrades were undertaken.

In this early 1990 photograph, the view looks down the driveway alongside 788 Ellicott Street. The Carriage House, built in the late 1800s, comes into view. This storage building would later be developed into supplementary apartments with the cooperation with Roswell Park Cancer Institute.

Here is a rear view of the Little Red School House building at the start of the reconstruction of the driveway in 1994. After the new concrete was installed, major structural upgrades were done to the rear of this house. These included a secondary two-floor extension off the back wall with insertion of multiple window units.

With the removal of the old concrete, the volunteer workers begin to set out the sight lines for the pouring of the new driveway. This image shows details of the original foundations and ground features of this late-1800s building.

The morning sun shines on Jen Ann Berger, former executive director of Kevin Guest House, following the installation of the new driveway between 782 and 788 Ellicott Street in 1994. Berger was responsible for implementing a new management system with new fundraising approaches for the house. She always credits Kevin for inspiration in securing resources to support "the mission."

The photograph above shows 788 Ellicott Street in August 2015, with another new color, shutters, contrasting trim, and landscaping. This major renovation of the Bone Marrow Transplant Apartment Building was made possible by generous support from the Margaret L. Wendt Foundation, with additional support from the Baird Foundation. Repairs to window frames and replacement of concrete in the Healing Garden were also included. The photograph below is the rear view of the structure. (Photographs by J.L. Smith, author's collection.)

This is the carriage apartments at 788½ Ellicott Street in August 2014. The original structure, built in the late 1800s, is in its 20th year of service to patients and families at Kevin Guest House. It will receive upgrades with handicap accessibility as the campus expands its facilities in 2016.

It is a beautiful day at the expanding Kevin Guest House campus on Ellicott Street in November 2015. The semicircular driveway provides easier access to the front entrance, which faces Ellicott Street. The street has seen a substantial increase in traffic as the surrounding Buffalo Niagara Medical Campus develops. (Photograph by Bill Sheff of Roswell Park Cancer Institute.)

Five

A MODEL FOR THE NATION

The charitable purpose of Kevin Guest House, as envisioned by the Garveys, was to provide guest house services so that other parents would not have to sleep in cars to be near their sick child. One of the greatest challenges for Cyril Garvey was to guide the Kevin Guest House committee from his home in Sharon, Pennsylvania. Despite his efforts, a serious financial crisis peaked in the early 1990s. It was proposed at that time that Kevin Guest House be closed. However, board members Neil Farmelo and Dean Drew devised a plan and asked for a six-month grace period to find a solution. The board of directors granted their request, and the plan succeeded. During the next 10 years, a new management system was implemented. A debt of gratitude is owed to Farmelo and Drew for their courage and commitment. The photograph features Drew and Jen Ann Berger, who was hired as the first executive director of Kevin Guest House.

Jen Ann Berger (left), executive director, and Carol Ann Reynolds, the resident manager of Kevin Guest House, leave for their first National Association of Hospital Hospitality Houses (NAHHH) convention in Nashville, Tennessee, in 1993. The theme for this event was "Kaleidoscope–National Hospital Hospitality Houses in the 90s." This national organization was incorporated in Michigan on February 18, 1986.

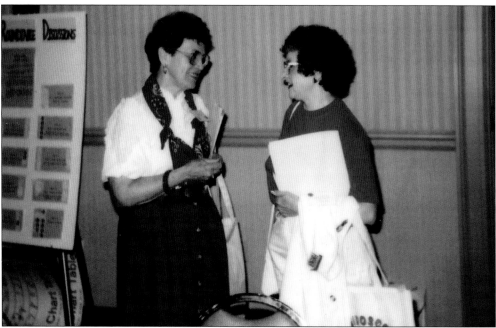

Kevin Guest House staff's active affiliation with the national organization created an opportunity to exchange ideas with other professionals from around the United States. Jen Ann Berger (right) speaks with a representative from Alabama at the 1993 National Association Hospital Hospitality House Convention. Berger recalled that this trip was the first long-distance drive she made without her husband, Wayne. She was determined that others throughout the nation learn about the work of Cyril and Claudia Garvey.

Kevin Guest House staff members, from left to right, Lyn Phinney, Jen Ann Berger, and Carol Ann Reynolds prepare to leave for their second National Association of Hospital Hospitality Houses National Conference in Columbus, Ohio, May 4–7, 1994. In the background is 766 Ellicott Street, which was destined to become part of the Kevin Guest House campus in 2015.

In May 1994, the National Association of Hospital Hospitality Houses, Inc., held its national conference in Columbus, Ohio. Its theme was "Discovery '94—Charting New Waters." The organization honored Cyril and Claudia Garvey with its recognition award for their founding of Kevin Guest House in July 1972. This image shows Cyril telling their story to the officers, members, and guests.

Gerry Beck was associated with the Beacon House in Marquette, Michigan. She was active on the national board and served as president of NAHHH in 1996 and 1997. Beck (far left) is seen here with, from left to right, Claudia Garvey, Cyril Garvey, and Ann-Marie Carroll.

From left to right, Lyn Phinney, Carol Ann Reynolds, Cyril Garvey, Claudia Garvey, and Jen Ann Berger proudly pose for a photograph following the ceremonies at the National Association of Hospital Hospitality Houses convention in Columbus, Ohio in 1994.

As the decades passed, the relationship between Roswell Park Cancer Institute and Kevin Guest House continued to strengthen. A commemoration ceremony at Roswell is shown with representatives of Kevin Guest House Board of Directors, staff, and employees of the hospital. From left to right are Mary Lou Boll, Aimee Gomlak, Henry Gorino, Kate Gordon, Jenn Ann Berger, Tom Surwill, Lyn Phinney, Fred Vosburgh, Lianne Reardon, Angela Bontempo, Jim Murphy, Maureen Hammond, Dean Drew, Amy Vigneron, Renee Paulson, Don Kloda, and Karen Synor. (Above, courtesy of Fred Vosburgh.)

This beautiful rendition of Kevin Guest House was painted by Marilyn Reynolds. It was presented to Roswell Park Cancer Institute on June 29, 1999, in a ceremony with members of the Kevin Guest House Board of Directors. Dr. M. Steven Piver, head of gynecologic oncology, accepted the painting on behalf of the hospital. From left to right are Dr. Piver, Marilyn Reynolds (the artist), Tom Surwill (member of the Kevin Guest House Board of Directors), and Jen Ann Berger.

Cyril Garvey's family recalled him saying, "If you are lucky enough to have just one good idea and work really hard on it, it makes life all worthwhile." Cyril's dedication to his family and personal struggle led to establishing Kevin Guest House. Having been awarded made a Knight of St. Gregory by Pope John Paul II and with a lifetime of service behind him, Cyril T. Garvey passed into his final reward on January 19, 1996. (Courtesy of Denis and Suzy Garvey.)

This is the original Ronald McDonald House, located at 4032 Spruce Street in West Philadelphia, Pennsylvania, in 1974. (Courtesy of Ronald McDonald House, Philadelphia, Pennsylvania.)

The Garveys' personal mission inspired others throughout the United States. The first Ronald McDonald House was founded in Philadelphia in 1974 by Dr. Audrey Evans and James Murray, formerly of the Philadelphia Eagles. Murray is mentioned in an article in the *Buffalo News* in 1983 in which he points out that Kevin Guest House was the model for their Philadelphia Hospital Hospitality House. (Courtesy of Ronald McDonald House, Philadelphia, Pennsylvania.)

The Ronald McDonald House of Charlotte, located at 1613 East Morehead Street in Charlotte, North Carolina, opened in May 2011. Denis and Suzy Garvey were invited and met James Murray at the ceremony. Murray introduced them to the McDonald's Corporation representatives by proclaiming that their family began the hospital hospitality movement in 1972 by opening the Kevin Guest House. From left to right are Denis Garvey, mascot Ronald McDonald, Suzy Garvey, and James Murray. (Above, courtesy of Ronald McDonald House of Charlotte, North Carolina; below, courtesy of Denis and Suzy Garvey.)

The Hospitality House of Charlotte, located at 1400 Scott Avenue in Charlotte, North Carolina, was founded in 1985 by a group of physicians' wives. It provides services for patients receiving treatments for serious health-related matters and their families. (Courtesy of Hospitality House of Charlotte, North Carolina.)

INDIG

Dear Mr. Garvey: October 21, 2002

I saw your cover story in the *South Charlotte Weekly* the day I returned home from Buffalo, New York, where I had attended the funeral of my oldest sister. She passed away after a long illness, and over these last six months, my family members have been frequent visitors at the Kevin Guest House. They speak with such gratitude about the warmth and compassion they found there during this difficult period!

We are a family of five girls, all raised in Buffalo. Four of us now live in North Carolina (three here in Charlotte and one in Boone). I couldn't believe the coincidence of picking up the paper and reading the background of your family's magnificent act of love, about which I had heard so much.

As I thought over the best way to express our gratitude, I realized that this year, our financial contributions would be limited by the fact that all of us virtually gave up our careers to be at my sister's side (one reason Kevin House was so important to us). So, for the time being, I'm writing to offer our service instead. Some of us may be more useful to you than others - for example, my sister in Boone is a professor of Early Childhood Development and my youngest sister in Charlotte is a dance instructor (tap, jazz, ballet etc.)...probably not much in-kind potential there! However, another sister is a real-time court reporter and I am a video writer/producer/editor.

I'd be delighted to assist your organization with a fund-raising or background video that could be available in all of the hospitality homes. Or another project of your choice. My sister's life was defined by simple acts of kindness and a prodigious power of memory - she never forgot a birthday, an anniversary, her family or her friends. It would mean so much to me to carry her legacy forward.

Sincerely,

Terry Losardo
Producer

Circumstances in life sometimes have a coincidental quality. Denis and Suzy Garvey were featured in an article in a Charlotte, North Carolina, neighborhood publication about their work with the Healthcare Hospitality Network in 2002. Terry Losardo found a copy of the paper at the bottom of her driveway the night she returned home from burying her sister in Buffalo. Her family had stayed at Kevin Guest House during her sister's final days. Soon after this letter was received, Losardo met the Garveys and began to volunteer, and later became a board member, at the Hospitality House of Charlotte. (Courtesy of Denis and Suzy Garvey.)

Buffalo, New York, is unique in having four hospitality houses renovated from Victorian Era homes. This includes the Ronald McDonald House on West Ferry Street; Grace House, which serves Mercy Hospital; and the Hope Lodge, at 197 Summer Street, shown in this photograph. Hope Lodge has a designated service for cancer patients. All these institutions are considered "sister charities." (Photograph by J.L. Smith, courtesy of Hope Lodge, Buffalo, New York.)

Kevin Guest House developed its own recognition of its volunteers, known as the Heart Award. Joanne Janicki, head of the Breast Resource Center at Roswell Park Cancer Institute, received the award at an Affaire of the Heart celebration. Janicki gave great service and truly opened her heart to the guests by coordinating the dinner program for decades. From left to right are former executive director Wayne Zimmerman, Janicki, and Suzy Garvey.

Seen here is the porch of the Grand Hotel on Mackinac Island, Michigan, in September 2002 at the National Association of Hospital Hospitality Houses, Inc., conference. The organization honored Claudia Garvey and her late husband, Cyril, on the 30th anniversary of the founding of Kevin Guest House. The Garveys' son Denis presented his mother with the association's prestigious ACORN Award. This association, now known as the Healthcare Hospitality Network, had a membership in 2015 of nearly 500 houses nationwide serving approximately 400,000 people each year. From left to right are (first row) Suzy Garvey, Claudia Garvey, and Annette Garvey Waymel; (second row) Hugh Garvey, Tom Garvey, Denis Garvey, John Garvey, and Steve Waymel. (Courtesy of Denis and Suzy Garvey.)

Claudia Garvey reminisced that losing Kevin was extremely difficult, but she and Cyril were determined to help others like those they met during their time in Buffalo. Claudia remarked that it was a wonderful thing that they had made it their life's work to help others in need. Claudia joined her husband, Cyril, on September 20, 2006. (Courtesy of Darlene Spychala.)

Six

HOME AWAY FROM HOME

In order to honor and respect the privacy of the more than 53,000 guests at Kevin Guest House, a small number of them have graciously shared their stories in this book. Remembered here are Harold and Leslies Menges of New Hartford, New York, on January 6, 1993. The Menges were guests at the Kevin Guest House following Harold's lifesaving heart transplant at Buffalo General Hospital. Until his death in August 2015, Harold was passionate in his promotion of organ donation.

Couple Ann Curtain and Frank Marletto met again after many years and had a unique experience at Kevin Guest House. After each lost a spouse, Curtain and Marletto unexpectedly saw each other following a medical appointment and began dating shortly after that. While staying at Kevin Guest House, Marletto spoke with Tom and Denis Garvey. To their mutual astonishment, it was discovered that Frank had grown up in Sharon, Pennsylvania, attended the same church as Tom's father, Cyril, and had lived relatively close to the Garvey home in his younger days.

Seated in the Healing Garden at Kevin Guest House, Ann Noble has been traveling from Binghamton, New York, for medical services at Roswell Park Cancer Institute for over 30 years. Noble wrote that when she walks through the doors at Kevin Guest House, she immediately feels "at home." Noble expresses the depth of her gratitude for the other guests. They willingly shared their personal stories, demonstrating strength and resiliency as they faced the challenges of personal medical issues. It is certain that others received a reciprocal gift from Noble.

The dinner program is a very important aspect at Kevin Guest House. It provides a special time for over 12,000 guests annually, prepared by volunteers and staff. Eating a family-style meal together in the dining room restores some normalcy to a schedule of medical appointments, often very far from home. Among those who prepare the meals is the group of friends known as the "Sangria Girls," who wear special aprons with colorful name tags. Their name comes from one of their favorite drinks enjoyed during the meals.

Seen here is Richie Segnit with his chef's hat in the kitchen of Kevin Guest House. He baked his delightful "mile-high pies" for Tom, Denis, and Suzy Garvey during the afternoon of an Affaire of the Heart fundraiser. Segnit was a notable guest who loved cars, loved to talk, and really loved to bake. Below, Richie is pictured with his vintage car that he parked in the garage at Kevin Guest House during his trips there. (Left, courtesy of Denis and Suzy Garvey.)

From Waddington, a small community in Upstate New York near the Canadian border, Brenda Stoner Dunning traveled to Buffalo in April 2012 to receive treatment at Roswell Park Cancer Institute. A suitable donor had been found for a bone marrow transplant, thus Brenda and her husband, Jim, stayed in bone marrow transplant apartments during several months. Brenda wrote that receiving expressions of genuine concern from the staff and other guests became a source of inspiration for her.

Pictured here, from left to right, are Cal and Glenda Walker of Ithaca, New York, with longtime friends Martha and Gerald Smith on the front porch of Kevin Guest House. Following treatments at Cayuga Hematology and Oncology Associates in Ithaca and a bone marrow/stem cell transplant at Roswell Park Cancer Institute, the Walkers have stayed at Kevin Guest House during Cal's posttransplant phase. He liked to spend long periods in the gazebo in the Healing Garden behind the main house—so much so that he referred to it as "my sanctuary" and looked forward to spending time there every day.

Nicholas and Barb Dixon from Duke Center, Pennsylvania, have been supported by the care and services at Kevin Guest House since December 2015. Their son, Nick Jr., has been receiving medical rehabilitation at Buffalo General Medical Center. They specifically expressed feelings of gratitude for the comfort received during the Dinner Program in the evenings during the week. (Photograph by J.L. Smith, author's collection.)

Amee Patel rushed her father to Buffalo, New York, from a hospital in Hamilton, Ontario, Canada, for emergency cardiac surgery at Buffalo General Hospital. She was accompanied by her mother, Snehalataben. Following her father's further health complications, Amee and her mother had a lengthy stay at Kevin Guest House. Although Snehalataben does not speak English, she prepared delicious Indian food that she warmly offered to the other guests and staff. Amee remarked that Kevin Guest House feels more like home than a hotel.

Blowing bubbles in front of the main house is guest Chuck McCann with his grandchildren Shane (right) and Zeland. Chuck's son Shawn was serving in the military and stationed at Fort Drum in New York State when he was sent to Roswell Park Cancer Institute for treatment of leukemia. During his son's extensive hospitalization, Chuck stayed at Kevin Guest House. He described it as his "normalizing" place. Although Chuck lost his son, he speaks with deep gratitude for the support he received from staff and other guests. Pictured at right is Chuck's son's family: from left to right, Zeland, Jennifer, Shawn, and Shane.

Sandy and Bruce Garthwaite are from Great Valley, New York, located south of Buffalo. As a patient of Roswell Park Cancer Institute, Sandy received a bone marrow transplant and, along with husband Bruce, stayed in the transplant recovery apartments at Kevin Guest House during 2014. Sandy recalled that it was wonderful to have their own apartment so that their children and grandchildren could visit and share a private meal together. Kevin Guest House's proximity to the hospital allowed the Garthwaites to quickly reach the treatment floor during the first 100 days of Sandy's recovery.

Both Carol Cole of Coudersport, Pennsylvania, and Morisa Fleming of Port Allegheny, Pennsylvania, had their respective husbands flown to Buffalo for emergency medical procedures. Cole and Fleming had similarly remarked that they felt "right at home" in the facility. Cole expressed her feelings, saying that "Kevin Guest House provided a comfortable, safe haven with genuine support from staff, volunteers and guests to cope with the unpredictable of the medical world." From left to right are Courtney Jensen, Cole, Kate Heidinger, Fleming, and Lynsey Zimdahl Weaver. (Photograph by J.L. Smith, author's collection.)

Seven

GIVING "HEART TO HEART"

Volunteers have always been the "lifeblood of the heart" of Kevin Guest House. Here, Jen Ann Berger, the first executive director, watches Michael DeMonaco (center) and Robert Jenkinson install cabinets in one of the apartments in September 1993. These volunteers were provided through special arrangements with Ford Motor Company. The materials were donated by the local Valu Home Centers. (Photograph by Robert L. Smith.)

The We Care Junior Gardeners, a youth group of the Orchard Park Garden Club, planted flowers at Kevin Guest House in June 1993. The volunteers were supervised by Carol Ann Reynolds, the first occupant of the new third-floor apartment in the main house. Here, the children enjoy a well-deserved break on the front porch of the main house.

Helping out with the daily operational chores at Kevin Guest House was the task of volunteers from the West Avenue Presbyterian Church of Buffalo on its designated day on July 28, 1993. The volunteers also performed simple repairs and baked treats for the guests.

The Nations First
Hospital Hospitality House

**KEVIN GUEST
HOUSE**

*Cordially invites you to
the first Annual*

**"AFFAIR OF
THE HEART"**

at the

DELAWARE PARK CASINO

Wednesday, September 28, 1994
7:00 o'clock in the evening

Donation:
$75.00 per person
($50.00 tax deductible)

To Benefit the
Kevin Guest House

№ 333

On September 28, 1994, the first Affaire of the Heart event was held at the Delaware Park Casino in Buffalo, New York. It had been 20 years since the first Kevin Ball was held at the Statler Hilton Hotel in downtown Buffalo on March 23, 1974. Jen Ann Berger is surrounded by guests from Alpha Omega Zeta, a coed fraternity from the State University College at Buffalo. From left to right are Pauline Skowron, John Aleksiejuk, Mike Gambino, and Melody Calabrese.

Student volunteers from the Culinary Arts Program at Emerson Vocational High School, part of Buffalo Public Schools, received food service training at Kevin Guest House during the 1996–1997 school year. Supervision and instruction was carried out by chef Rebecca Formwalt. The meals were prepared in the kitchen and later served, while the students wore their signature red blazers. Students also did maintenance during the morning or afternoon, and the program supervision was conducted by Carol Ann Reynolds. (Courtesy of Chef Rebecca Formwalt.)

Volunteers take on the task of painting the retaining wall behind the bone marrow transplant apartment building at Kevin Guest House. This photograph was taken on the United Way Day of Caring in 1998.

Beryl Szatkowski, originally from England, was the first volunteer at Kevin Guest House. Following the death of her son, Szatkowski answered an advertisement in the *Buffalo News* for a volunteer. She later became the volunteer coordinator, working with 23 volunteers. Szatkowski is remembered for her sunny disposition along with her ability to recruit others to volunteer.

Longtime volunteer Roz Annunizato helps cultivate an interest in the history of the property by leading her tours of Kevin Guest House as Mathilda Speyser-Beer, dressed in beautiful clothing of an earlier era. Her artistic interpretation of the buildings, the Fruit Belt neighborhood, and the creation of the guest house is truly appreciated by guests and visitors alike. With her love of Kevin Guest House and her skills as an educator, Annunizato's personal research has served as a major resource for the material presented in this book. The author is indebted to Annunizato for her support and guidance throughout the research process.

Each July, staff, volunteers, guests, and friends celebrate the founding of Kevin Guest House with an anniversary open house. This is the front yard with the familiar red-and-white-striped tent on July 26, 2000. Among those attending that day were Robert Beer, his wife, Florence, and their grandchildren Abby and John Rodgers. Robert's presence is significant because he assisted in the negotiations for the sale of his parent's home to Cyril Garvey. On his visits to the house, Robert would provide details about the Speyser-Beer family's history and memories of his childhood.

For over 20 years, golf events have supported Kevin Guest House. The Celebrity Golf Classic in 2015 featured, from left to right (first row) Kevyn Adams, Patrick Kane, Terry Martin, and Kevin O'Connell; (second row) Don Luce, Rene Robert, Harry Neale, Kevin Sylvester, John Koelmel, Bob Mellon, Danny Gare, and Michael Peca; (third row) Justin Bailey, Zach Bogosian, Cody McCormick, Andrew Peters, Pete Ratchuk, Dave Leggio, Booker Edgerson, and Lou Piccone.

Players from the Buffalo Sabres hockey organization have shown support for Kevin Guest House for many years. At the 2015 Affaire of the Heart, the young hockey star Jack Eichel of the Sabres donated a jersey for auction at the annual fundraising event in 2015. The high bid was offered by Michael and Darlene Spychala, shown here with the Eichel jersey. Darlene is a former member of the board of directors and longtime supporter of Kevin Guest House. The event was held in the Mary Seaton Room at Kleinhans Music Hall in Buffalo. (Photograph by J.L. Smith, author's collection.)

The JPMorgan Chase Corporate Challenge is held annually on a Thursday evening in June in Delaware Park in Buffalo. In 2015, approximately 12,375 runners and walkers from 396 companies covered the three-and-a-half-mile course. The time honored event supports Kevin Guest House and the Angel Fund of Roswell Park Cancer Institute, which provides funds to patients for assistance in travel and lodging expenses. From left to right are David Horan (of JPMorgan Chase), Buffalo mayor Byron Brown, Olympian Steve Mesler, Fred Vosburgh and Bill Dehmer (both of JPMorgan Chase), Roswell Institute physician Dr. Killian Salerno, and Lynsey Weaver (of Kevin Guest House).

Western New York running enthusiasts have supported Kevin Guest House with the help of the Checkers Running Club for over 19 years. Tom Donnelly served as its president and was instrumental in developing Kevin Guest House's long-standing relationship with John Noe and Mueller Services, which sponsored the annual Mueller Mile. Donnelly's sudden passing was a loss to his family, the staff at Kevin Guest House, and the local running community. This photograph of Donnelly and Wendy Guyker was taken in 2012.

Local businesses provide volunteers to perform a variety of tasks for Kevin Guest House throughout the year. Here, a crew from National Grid stopped by to decorate the main house with lights to help lift the spirits of the guests at Christmastime.

A group of volunteers from Kaleida Health and the Erie County Industrial Development Agency worked to install a new wooden fence along the retaining wall behind the bone marrow transplant apartment building at Kevin Guest House in August 2015. This ambitious project included grounds maintenance along Kevin's Way, next to the main parking lot.

Many local churches have sent volunteers to help out at Kevin Guest House as part of their community-outreach ministry. These volunteers from the Well church in Buffalo did some gardening and yard cleanup.

This is the charismatic team of young volunteers from the Community Active People Program of People, Inc., of Western New York. Under the guidance of instructor Kelly McEachon, the team helps out with weekly housekeeping duties. From left to right are (first row) Larry, Jenny, Denise, and Kelly; (second row) Chris and Christian.

Teacher Joy Blake and her eighth-grade students from Buffalo Academy of Science Charter School volunteer to help with the seasonal outside chores at Kevin Guest House. Many schools have their students participate with nonprofit organizations as part of community-based learning curriculums and to encourage volunteerism.

Under the coordination of Paul E. O'Leary, Deloitte employees swarm the Healing Garden of Kevin Guest House as part of a Deloitte Impact Day in 2014. The dynamic volunteers in signature blue T-shirts help with the seasonal needs of the garden.

The "I Paid It Forward" campaign sign is held proudly by Ron Burgouis, pictured with, from left to right, Chris McNamara, Liz Pinapento, and Jonathan Olsen at the Roswell Appreciation Event held in the Healing Garden at Kevin Guest House. This program was inspired by guests who wanted to "pay it forward" for other guests who were struggling financially.

In June 2015, while attending a reunion of the Hotel Company, 2nd Battalion, 7th Marines in Buffalo, New York, Jerry Norris's wife, Ann, became ill. Through the kindness of a nurse at Buffalo General Medical Center, Jerry was referred to Kevin Guest House. This handwritten letter expresses his feelings about his experiences during Ann's medical treatments. Jerry spent 23 nights at Kevin Guest House.

Dear friends,

I once heard someone say, "People make plans and God laughs".

My wife and I were excited to make our first trip to Buffalo for a reunion of fellow Marines from Vietnam, with whom I served. While here, my wife became ill and was admitted to the ICU at Buffalo General Medical Center with acute pneumonia and a couple of days turned into weeks. Not being financially able to afford a hotel, I sought out alternatives. A very kind and helpful nurse suggested Kevin Guest House, even calling to make my reservation.

Being nearly 1400 miles from our home in Wichita Falls, Texas, I did not know what to expect. I was welcomed and immediately put at ease by the kind and wonderful staff; Lynsey, Pam, Andrew, Kate and Jeff. The people of Buffalo and those traveling here in need of medical care are truly blessed to have this home away from home.

As I write this, I am in the ICU with my wife of 42 years and was told by doctors to expect the worst, thus the old saying, "People make plans and God laughs". We planned a few days of vacation, but he had different plans.

Thank you to all of you who help support Kevin Guest House - this house has a heart larger than Texas, and that says it all. Please consider a donation and "pay it forward" for someone else in need.

God Bless Kevin Guest House and Staff.

Jerry L. Norris
Wichita Falls, Texas

The Roswell Appreciation Day was created to express thanks and give recognition to employees of Roswell Park Cancer Institute for the decades of support to Kevin Guest House. Tom Garvey had the distinct honor of introducing the featured guest speaker, Dr. Candace Johnson, the president and CEO of Roswell Park Cancer Institute. Dr. Johnson emphatically spoke of the important relationship between the medical services and guest services provided by Kevin Guest House. (Photograph by J.L. Smith, author's collection.)

Roswell employees Jill Kaczor (left) and her sister Colleen Sarick enjoy themselves in the Healing Garden during the Roswell Recognition Event at Kevin Guest House. (Photograph by J.L. Smith, author's collection.)

The annual Oktoberfest event was held in the Kaminski Park green space on the grounds of the Roswell Park Cancer Institute during the evening of September 18, 2015. The festive celebration featured live music, beers and wine, and fine arts from many local brewers and artisans.

Courtney Jensen, house manager and volunteer coordinator, and her family are pictured at Oktoberfest in October 2015 on Roswell Hospital grounds. From left to right are Courtney, Mark SanFilipo, Ann Marie Pozorski, Diane Pozorski, Jack Jensen, Holly Maloney, and Patrick Maloney.

Blues & Brews fundraiser at the Ellicott Square Building in 2012 featured Jack Civiletto with "Win, Lose or Draw." Originally described as a "friend-raiser" by Al Ryer, this rousing musical evening is a complement to the Oktoberfest. (Photograph by Michael Argento, courtesy of Argento Photography.)

This image was captured during the Affaire of the Heart celebration at the Statler Hilton Hotel in Buffalo. Since its inception in 1994, many fine establishments throughout Western New York have hosted this important annual fundraising event, such as the Mary Seaton Room at Kleinhans Music Hall and Salvatore's Italian Gardens.

Throughout the years, many of the finest young local musicians have graced the stage at the annual Affaire of the Heart events. St. Joe's Jazz Band from St. Joseph's Collegiate Institute in Kenmore, New York, performs at the 2015 Affaire of the Heart at Kleinhans Music Hall in Buffalo. (Photograph by J.L. Smith, author's collection.)

Members of the Garvey family came to Buffalo to join the November 13, 2015, celebration to support Kevin Guest House, which was founded by their parents. Joining members of the board of directors in the hallway outside the Mary Seaton Room of Kleinhans Music Hall at the Affaire of the Heart are, from left to right, Tom Garvey, Mary Garvey, Karen Durawa, Lynsey Zimdahl-Weaver (executive director), Kevin Durawa (president of the board), Suzy Garvey, and Denis Garvey. (Photograph by J.L. Smith, author's collection.)

Eight

EXPANDING SERVICES
FOR THE FUTURE

This Second Empire mansion at 766 Ellicott Street in Buffalo will serve as the foundation for the expansion of services at the Kevin Guest House in 2016. The building was constructed in 1866 by John Irlbacher. Later, in 1906, August Feine, a German immigrant, purchased the house, enhancing it with his skills as a wrought-iron ornamental craftsman. The most recent owners—Schröder, Joseph & Associates—sold the property to Kevin Guest House to allow the original campus to be expanded. (Photograph by Bill Sheff of Roswell Park Cancer Institute, courtesy of Kevin Guest House.)

This aerial view shows the recently acquired building at 766 Ellicott Street in relation to the original buildings that comprise the Kevin Guest House campus. Somewhat obscured by the trees is Kevin's Way, running alongside the main parking lot next to the (blue) main house to the right. The bone marrow transplant apartment building is just visible at the extreme right. (Photograph by Bill Sheff of Roswell Park Cancer Institute, courtesy of Kevin Guest House.)

This excellent photograph shows the horizon toward the west, with the Niagara River bordering Canada in the distance. This is one of the massive cranes on the framework of the new University at Buffalo Jacobs School of Medicine and Biomedical Sciences, the structure immediately behind Kevin Guest House campus; it is scheduled to open in 2017. (Photograph by Bill Sheff of Roswell Park Cancer Institute, courtesy of Kevin Guest House.)

This view facing south of the KGH campus shows Ellicott Street running toward downtown Buffalo. Just to the left of 766 Ellicott Street (redbrick building), the dark brown building of St. Jude's Center can be seen. This religious haven is often used by guests staying at Kevin Guest House. (Photograph by Bill Sheff of Roswell Park Cancer Institute, courtesy of Kevin Guest House.)

When guests approach the newly acquired mansion from the driveway at street level, the unique appointments of pediments, tall windows, custom ironwork, and the solarium can be appreciated. (Photograph by Monica Bruce, author's collection.)

The grand front door of 766 Ellicott Street is seen here with its distinct black wrought-iron trim work. This building will increase the guest capacity, which is a reflection of the demand for services provide through the growth of Buffalo Niagara Medical Campus. While over 1,200 guests are served each year, about 400 families per year are turned away, unfortunately. This expansion will allow service for 24 more guests per day. (Photograph by Monica Bruce, author's collection.)

This is a close-up view of the house number embedded within the foliage motif and the lower door panel on the front door of 766 Ellicott Street. Along with access through this strong, heavy door, future guests with acute medical needs or disabilities will also have access to an elevator. This service will be available for the first time in Kevin Guest House history. (Photograph by Monica Bruce, author's collection.)

Through the front entranceway, this stairway leads up to the second floor. The wood carving in the banister and railings complement the exterior wrought ironwork. (Photograph by Monica Bruce, author's collection.)

After entering the hallway, the beautiful storm door is visible. All Kevin Guest House associates and the Garvey family are very grateful to Linda Joseph and Ginger Schröder for their commitment and generosity in offering this elegant mansion for expansion of the campus. (Photograph by Monica Bruce, author's collection.)

The interior rooms of the first floor have characteristically high ceilings, tall windows, parquet floors, marble fireplaces, corbeils, wide trim moulding, and pocket doors with handcrafted pulls and latches. Renovations to the first floor will include a multipurpose room, kitchenette, and a handicap-accessible private bathroom. Also, one larger suite will be designed for larger families. (Photograph by J.L. Smith, author's collection.)

An evening event was held in November 2015 to have former members of the Kevin Guest House Board of Directors tour the newly acquired building at 766 Ellicott Street. It was an opportunity for many of them to interact with each other after many years and to hear about the plans for the campus expansion. (Author's collection.)

Fred Vosburgh of JPMorgan Chase, a former board president, and Amy Vigneron, of Cohen & Lombardo P.C., served on the board during the same period. Here, they share a laugh at the reunion event.

Former board members at the reunion event gather on the porch at Kevin Guest House in November 2015. From left to right are John Zimmerman, Debbie Zimmerman, Marge Palowski, Steve McGlone, Frank DelSignore, and Glenn Palkowski.

Former president of the Kevin Guest House Board of Directors Dean Drew (left) is pictured with Tom Garvey at the reunion event in November 2015.

In order to maintain its mission, Kevin Guest House must serve the community's major health care institutions with a unified spirit of cooperation. The responsibility for this falls to the leadership. Throughout its 44-year history, it has been the Garvey family; the Roswell Park Cancer Institute administration, employees, and volunteers; and the staff, volunteers, and donors of Kevin Guest House at the root of this mission of service. This memorable photograph symbolizes this essence. From left to right are Tom Garvey, son of the founders; Dr. Candace Johnson, president and CEO of Roswell; and Lynsey Weaver, executive director. (Photograph by J.L. Smith, author's collection.)

Cyril T. Garvey and Claudia Evans Garvey were the founders of Kevin Guest House. Their personal work and vision is being carried forward through time. To help achieve this, Cyril found meaning in these words of Mother Teresa: "Unless life is lived for others it is not worthwhile." With the expansion of the Kevin Guest House campus in 2016, supported by all who grasp the spirit of its mission, the service will always be there for those who come to Kevin's house.

Discover Thousands of Local History Books
Featuring Millions of Vintage Images

Arcadia Publishing, the leading local history publisher in the United States, is committed to making history accessible and meaningful through publishing books that celebrate and preserve the heritage of America's people and places.

Find more books like this at
www.arcadiapublishing.com

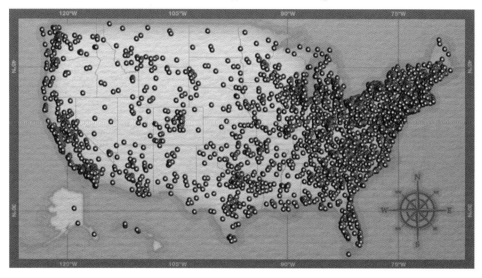

Search for your hometown history, your old stomping grounds, and even your favorite sports team.

Consistent with our mission to preserve history on a local level, this book was printed in South Carolina on American-made paper and manufactured entirely in the United States. Products carrying the accredited Forest Stewardship Council (FSC) label are printed on 100 percent FSC-certified paper.

MADE IN THE USA